READAND C

FACTS FOR THE PEOPLE!

ADDRESS OF THE

Rep. Central Committee

OF INGHAM COUNTY.

To the People of the State of Michigan—

STATE ISSUES.

The leaders of the pro-slavery Democracy, sensible that they cannot maintain a contest with the Republican party upon the National questions at issue between the parties, seek to divert the attention of the people of Michigan to questions of State policy and finance.

Through a reckless misrepresentation of the purpose and policy of the Republican party; by means of a careful concealment of some of the features of that policy, and a gross distortion of others; by falsehoods, slanders and libels, they hope to delude the people into the mistaken belief that the Republican party, in the administration of the State government for the past five years, have been guilty of mismanagement, profligacy, and an utter disregard of the interests of the State.

These are grave charges, and would render any party against whom they are sustained, unworthy of your confidence or support.

A candid and truthful investigation of the facts in the case, will, to an intelligent mind, triumphantly vindicate the Republican party from the charges preferred against it.

To this investigation we invite our fellow citizens, appealing to records which cannot be disproved for the facts and figures we present.

The causes of present embarrassment lie back of Republican administrations. They had their origin in the reckless expenditure of many hundreds of thousands of dollars of borrowed capital upon useless works of "internal improvement," for the benefit of party jobbers and contractors, by which the State became burdened with an enormous public debt, and from which not a particle of benefit was ever derived; in untold sums stolen from the treasury by partizan favorites, or given away to them upon fraudulent claims or upon the most paltry pretexts; in appropriating to private or party purposes taxes levied expressly to pay the interest upon the State debt, and suffering the interest thereon to remain unpaid; in permitting large cash balances to lie in the treasury of the State almost without interest, that State officials might grow rich from their loan to banks and other corporations; in squandering the proceeds of the Trust Funds, while the building of necessary State institutions was utterly neglected; in creating scores of Wild-Cat Banks that drove a healthy currency out of every artery of trade and commerce, and supplied its place with worthless rags; and in the general policy of the democratic party, of which these are but instances—a policy stubbornly persisted in through all the long, dark years of their sway—whereby the settlement of the country, the development of its resources, and its growth in wealth and population were materially retarded.

The Republican party have striven earnestly to remedy the chronic evils inflicted upon the State by the frauds and mismanagement of their predecessors. Upon their accession to power, they promptly stopped the interest upon the unadjusted portion of the five million loan, which had accumulated to nearly a million of dollars, and remained unpaid. They at once passed a law requiring the State Treasurer to obtain interest at five per cent. on all loans of cash balances in the treasury; thus realizing from this source over *seventy thousand dollars in five years*, whereas the only omount ever paid in by the Democratic party for the use of the large sum constantly kept on hand, was the paltry pittance of $1,553 86.

They have promptly paid the interest upon the State debt, and reduced the principal as far as means were in their power. They have built up our State Institutions, and made them the pride and ornament of Michigan.

They have applied the resources derived from the sale of the Swamp Lands to opening up the wilderness for settlement, and have given free homes to indigent actual settlers; and by providing for the completion of the Geological Survey of the State; and by the appointment of an Emigrant Agency; as well as by the general scope of their legislation, they have subserved the best interests of Michigan, and have laid the foundation of her prosperity in the future.

To the general charges that are made agains us, we propose to make specific rejoinders, and prove by undeniable testimony the falsehood of the accusations,

But in order to show the obstacles with which the Republicans, as a party, have had to contend, as well as to contrast their policy with that of the Democratic party, it is necessary to begin with the early financial history of Michigan.

ORIGIN OF THE STATE DEBT—DEMOCRATIC RULE.

No State ever came into the Union with brighter prospects than Michigan. Possessing a good climate, a fertile soil, immense lumber resources and inexhaustible mineral wealth, and being penetrated by numerous navigable rivers, and surrounded by more than 3,000 miles of lake coast, her advantages were extraordinary, and with proper management of her financial affairs, would have soon placed her, in wealth and population, in the front rank of States. But unfortunately the interests of the State were committed to the hands of most reckless and extravagant men, who at once embarked in schemes the wildest and most absurd.

The State was without commerce, and almost destitute of population ; yet three lines of railroad were projected across it, and heavy appropriations made for their completion. Large appropriations were also made for the improvement of rivers whose navigation was valueless, and in opening canals through regions, some portions of which are even yet inhabited only by wolves and wild cats.

As the State had no resources, it was compelled to borrow. So the Democratic party effected the Five Million Loan, $2,342,960 of which (the only portion ever received by the State) was expended, squandered, lost or stolen, in carrying on this "grand scheme" of Internal Improvements. Like all lotteries, while a few drew prizes, the mass of the people drew blanks, and poverty and ruin were the consequence.

In addition to the State debt thus originated, the General Government in 1841 granted the State 500,000 acres of land at a minimum value of $625,000, for Internal Improvement purposes. No sooner had this grant been confirmed, than the cormorants who had already fattened upon the State, seized upon and "appropriated" it, and it disappeared at once into the vortex whither it had been preceded by the $5,000,000 loan.

The "closing out" of this transaction is thus commented upon by Gov. Barry, in his message of 1850, (page 14): "The Internal Improvement Lands are no longer a source of revenue. The large, if not wasteful appropriations by the Legislature of 1848 *not only included the residue then remaining, but also a large quantity previously disposed of.* The appropriations then made, amounting in the aggregate to 186,000 acres, *produced but inconsiderable good*, while at the same time, they absorbed $232,500 of the resources of the State, being a sum equal to the minimum price of the lands, for which they would have been sold, *and for which provision must be made by direct taxation.*"

Yet these spendthrifts and robbers, whose policy was to enrich themselves by fleecing the people, have the effrontery to cry out against the Republican party for making the necessary appropriations for building up State institutions which they neglected, and for applying the resources of the State for the liquidation of debts contracted by them.

In the fall of 1846, the Central and Southern Roads were sold, and the sums received on these sales were applied toward the extinguishment of that portion of the State debt known as the "Debt of the Internal Improvement Fund."

Gov. Felch. in his message to the Legislature of 1847, (page 4,) states the "total of Internal Improvement debt," after deducting the "balance due on the sale of the Central and Southern Railroads," to be $1,987,140.77, which, of course, was the amount sunk in the "internal improvements" made by the Democratic party, as the balance of these works were not worth the parchment upon which the contract for their sale might be written.

The following is a

TABLE *showing some of the items of losses to the State on works of internal improvement from* 1838 *to* 1847, *inclusive:*

			Dead Loss.
*Clinton and Kalamazoo Canal (abandoned),			$375,000 00
*Saginaw and Bad River Canal	do		52,749 98
*Northern Railroad	do		80,229 63
*Laplaisance Bay Railroad	do		34,113 00
*Improvement of State Salt Springs	do		35,970 16
* " St. Joseph River	do		26,797 72
* " Grand, Maple and Kalamazoo Rivers (abandoned),			32,775 25
Cost of M. C. R. R. (Felch's messages, 1846 and 1847,)		$2,382,797 97	
Proceeds of sale of M. C. R. R.,		2,000,000 00	
			382,797 97
Cost of M. S. R. R. (Ransom's message, 1849,)		$1,200,000 00	
Proceeds of sale of M. S. R. R.,		500,000 00	
			700,000 00
Total loss on these items alone,			$1,720,433 71

*See Barry's message of 1842, and subsequent messages and reports of Board of Internal Improvement.

It is proper, however, that we should acknowledge such credits to these works as we find upon the record. In Joint Doc. No. 4, 1847, (page 21,) David Shook, Superintendent of the Clinton and Kalamazoo Canal, states the amount of tolls received upon the canal to be $43.42. Also, in Joint Doc No. 4, 1849, (page 3,) there is the following

INVENTORY *of property now on hand belonging to the St. Joseph River Improvement:*

2 boats, 11 bed-ticks, 2 pails, 4 pieces of chain, 1 scraper, 5 pair hooks, 2 bars iron, 4 cranks, 2 lines (old), 2 cross-cut saws, 3 blocks, 1 hand-saw, 2 axes, 1 box old iron, 1 box dishes, 2 shovels, 1 anchor, 2 jugs, 2 poles, 1 tin horn, 1 rake, 24 blankets, 1 snatch block, 1 keel boat (Hoosier), 1 scrape boat, 1 towel, 6 bed-ticks, 10 quilts, 3 blankets, 2 axes, 1 1¾ inch auger, 1 stove and trimmings, 12 earthen plates, 2 earthen dishes, 20 knives and forks, 3 large spoons, 2 pot pails, 2 stone jugs, 1 large tin pan, 11 tea-spoons, 5 bowls, 16 cups and saucers, 2 pepper boxes, 1 stone jar, 2 tin pails, 2 tin dippers, 2 candlesticks, 2 pie pans, 2 coffee-pots, 1 tea canister, 1 wash-dish, 1 pair blocks and fall, 74 lbs. 3-inch rope, 69 lbs. 2½ inch rope, 200 ft. 5-inch rope (old), 40 ft. 4-inch rope (old), 1 buck-saw, 1 bow saw, 2 pair stone-hooks, 2 crow-bars, 2 socket pods (long), 5 socket pods (short).

JOHN F. PORTER,
Sup't St. Joseph River.

Such was the origin of the chief portion of the State debt, which still presses heavily upon the people of Michigan, and such were the objects for which it was incurred.

The following is the proportion of the debt of the Internal Improvement Fund to the total State debt, as given by Auditor General D. V. Bell, in his report of Dec. 1st, 1846 (Joint Doc. No. 2, 1847, page 23):

AGGREGATE INDEBTEDNESS OF THE STATE.

Debt of the General Fund,	$ 311,909 75
Debt of the Internal Improvem't Fund,	1,987,140 77
Total Debt,	$2,299,050 52

Aggregate resources applicable to its payment:

Resources of the General Fund	$389,275 01
do. internal improvement Fund	422,123 00
Total Resources	$811,398 01

As we have already seen, the available resources of the Internal Improvement Fund were squandered by the Legislature of 1848.

We cannot ascertain that the resources of the General Fund were ever applied upon the debt, but if they were, it follows that the entire State debt is due to the amount squandered upon Internal Improvements by a party professing at the same time to be opposed to the doctrine that either the National or State Governments should engage in any general system of Internal Improvements.

We submit that it ill becomes a party, who have been guilty of such astounding profligacy and recklessness in the management of the affairs of the State, to impugn the integrity of the Republican party because of expenditures necessarily incurred, and which have been made a burden by previous mismanagement and neglect.

Do you desire, fellow citizens, to reinstate a party in power, which in former times proved so recreant to its trusts?—We believe not.

But the exhibit we have given only discloses a portion of the losses incurred by the people of Michigan under this grand Democratic 'internal improvement' swindle.

Scores of claims for damages sustained by contractors, and others connected with these works, have been allowed by the Board of State Auditors, and paid.—Here is a specimen:

"Allowed by the Board, Dec. 2, 1854.

"Gilbert & Co., damages by reason of misrepresentation of the Commissioner of Internal Improvement made to induce a low bidding on letting contract on Clinton and Kalamazoo Canal....$2,204.29"

" Dec 30, 1854. Bronson Ingalls & Co., claim for damages (as above) $6,234 78"

These sums amount to many thousands of dollars.

But vast amounts of money were lost in other ways. Of the amount originally received on the five million loan, $600,000 were deposited in the Michigan State Bank and lost; $30,000 were carried off by an absconding agent of the Southern Railroad, and other sums, too numerous to mention, were lost, that never saw the light of official reports. There were also transactions of a different character. Here is one instance. In 1838 a loan of $100,000, for twenty years, was made by the State for the relief of the Detroit and Pontiac Railroad Company, and ample security for the payment of the principal and interest thereon was taken upon the stock and fixtures of the road. Only the first semi-annual installment of interest was paid by the Company, and in 1848, ten years afterwards, the then Attorney General, Geo. V. N. Lothrop, compromised the entire debt for $32,000, at an absolute loss to the State of $185,000. This same Lothrop is the Democratic candidate for Congress in the First Congressional District of the State.

But let us now pass to the consideration of the

STATE DEBT SINCE 1847.

As the pro-slavery Democracy would gladly repudiate the policy of their party in the matter of the State debt prior to

1847, just as they repudiated the unpaid portion of the five million loan, and just as they seek to repudiate the profligate and corrupt administration of James Buchanan; and as they claimed that *the* Democratic policy commenced with that period, we will trace the history of the State debt from that time until an outraged and indignant people hurled the Democratic party from power; and compare their record with that of the Republican party.

DEMOCRATIC INCREASE OF THE STATE DEBT IN 7 YEARS.

Auditor Gen. D. V. Bell, in his Report of Dec 1, 1847, (page 19,) states the "Total State Debt, for which she is liable without contingency," to be $2,290,768 51

Auditor General Swegles, in his Report of Dec. 1, 1854, (page 7.) makes the "Total funded and fundable Debt," ---------------------------------- 2,531,545 70

Democratic increase in 7 years, --- $240,777 19

REPUBLICAN DECREASE OF THE STATE DEBT IN 5 YEARS.

State Debt, Dec. 1, 1854, (Swegle's Report) $2,531,545 70

Auditor General Case, in his Report of Dec. 30, 1859, (page 11,) gives the Total State Indebtedness as --------- 2,316,328 94

Republican decrease in 5 years, ----$215,216 76

Notwithstanding this evidence, furnished principally by Democratic records, there are not wanting those who have the hardihood to declare that the "Democratic policy was constantly to diminish the State debt," and that the Republican party have largely increased it!

The exhibit we have given does not include the accretions to the Trust Funds, but pertains exclusively to the bonded debt of the State.

The relations of the Trust Funds to the State are entirely different from those of the bonded debt. The latter consists of loans made, usually for twenty years, the interest payable semi-annually, and the principal payable at the close of the period for which the loan was made, or "at any time thereafter, or at any time previous, at the option of the State."

It is plain, then, that this debt is under the direct control of the State government, and may be increased or diminished according to the means or necessities of the State. But with the Trust Funds the case is different. These are funds arising principally from the proceeds of the sale of lands "granted by the United States to the State, *for educational purposes*, and the proceeds of all lands or other property given by individuals, or appropriated by the State for like purposes," which the constitution declares "shall be and remain a PERPETUAL FUND," the interest and income of which "shall be inviolably appropriated and anually applied to the specific objects of the original gift, grant or appropriation."

Hence, the increase of the debt to the Trust Funds is no argument against the economy of an administration, or the prudence with which it has managed the affairs of the State. The only manner in which this increase can be prevented is by robbery of these sacred inheritances of the people. In this, as in other instances, the Democracy have availed themselves of their prerogative of plundering the State, as the following exhibit from the School Laws of Michigan—a work issued in 1859, by the Superintendent of Public Instruction, will show:

Table showing the amount lost to the Primary School and University Funds during Democratic rule.

Deficiency in the Primary School Fund [see school laws, page 19], ----------------------	$ 34,234 65
Worthless loans of Primary School Fund, [see School Laws, page 18] -------------	11,900 00
Deficiency in the University Fund [see School Laws, page 57], ----------------	25,590 51
Total, -------------------------------	$71,725 16

Thus we see that the Democratic party, besides the vast amount it has plundered from other sources, has been guilty of a most culpable robbery of **$71,725 16!** from funds made forever sacred to the youth of Michigan, by the constitution of the State! Fellow citizens do you wish to return to this *Democratic policy?* If so, vote the Democratic ticket.

But to return. We have shown by their own records that the Democratic party, during the last seven years of its sway—a period pointed to with pride as illustrating, par excellence, Democratic State policy—increased the State debt $240,777 19. When, therefore, they assert that "the Democratic policy was constantly to diminish the State debt," they state a willful and deliberate falsehood.

But what apology can they offer for this increase? None whatever. They did not expend the resources of the State on works of internal improvement, (with the exception of *finishing*, in 1848, the grant of land made by Congress for that purpose, and paying old debts,) because these works had already been sold or abandoned. Neither did they apply these resources to building up State Institutions, for they left this work for the Republican party to perform. They will hardly desire to claim that this increase was made necessary to meet the ordinary expenses of the government, and on account of sums squandered or stolen from the treasury by themselves, yet we defy them to show that this sum was devoted to any honest expenditure whatever.

The Republican party, on the other hand, besides reducing the State debt $215,216 76, as shown by the Auditor General's reports, have paid a much larger amount of interest accruing thereon than was paid during the Democratic period referred to—have met the increasing expenditures consequent upon a growing State, and have paid a much larger sum for the development of the resources of the State and the building up of its institutions ; while all these have been done with less aggregate receipts than were those of the seven previous years of Democratic rule. The following table exhibits the receipts from all sources for the following years :

DEMOCRATIC PERIOD (SEVEN YEARS).

Cash on hand Dec. 1,	1847,	$ 62,304 45
Receipts of	1848,	360,868 57
"	1849,	494,165 06
"	1850,	429,268 28
"	1851,	352,517 22
"	1852,	451,082 97
"	1853,	655,667 86
"	1854,	610,699 97
Total..............		$3,416,574 33

REPUBLICAN PERIOD (FIVE YEARS).

Cash on hand, Jan. 1,	1855,	$ 468,893 39
Receipts of	1855,	588,396 93
"	1856,	511,271 70
"	1857,	450,653 85
"	1858,	668,720 00
"	1859,	704,006 02
Total..............		$3 392,941 89

RECAPITULATION.

Total receipts of Democratic period,	$3,416.574 38
ditto of Repub. period,	3,392,941 89
Democratic excess,	$23,632 49

This showing is too favorable to the Democratic party, as in the receipts of 1859 is included the loan of $100,000 made for the repairs of the St. Mary's Falls Ship Canal.

By reference to the amount of cash on hand Dec. 1, 1847, it will be seen that there have been occasions under Democratic rule when there was a far less amount in the treasury than at any time under Republican rule. Let us now compare the expenditures during these periods, and first, let us look at the interest paid upon the State debt.

TABLE showing the interest paid upon the State debt, with the exchange thereon, from 1848 to 1859 inclusive.

Dem. period (7 years).		Rep. period (5 years).	
1848,	$50.124 87	1855,	$54,141 66
1849,	83.501 30	1856,	91,020 29
1850,	52.522 65	1857,	129,134 60
1851,	54,051 11	1858,	135,733 87
1852,	56,495 29	1859,	134,208 21
1853,	72,060 28		
1854,	56,304 26	Total,	$544,238 63
Total,	$425,059 76		

RECAPITULATION.

Interest paid by Reprblicans in 5 years,	$544,238 63
" " " Democrats in 7 years,	425,059 76
Republican excess,	$119.178 87

ORDINARY EXPENSES.

The following table comprises payments of the principal of the State debt, (except Internal Improvement Warrants and Warrant Bonds,) interest disbursed from the educational trust funds, expenses of the tax-paying department, the Judiciary, the State prison, the Legislature, printing, binding, &c., salaries of public officers, stationery for public offices, and sundry minor expenditures :

Dem. period (7 years).		Rep. period (5 years)	
1848,	$206,032 99	1855,	$354,982 42
1849,	241,559 21	1856,	406,530 41
1850,	267,493 75	1857,	366,278 15
1851,	252,322 14	1858,	375.786 64
1852,	356,352 63	1859,	419,168 85
1853,	301,080 35		
*1854,	353,911 38	Total,	$1,922,746 47
Total,	$1,978,752 45		

RECAPITULATION.

Expenses of Democratic period,	$1,978,752 45
" Republican "	1,922,746 47
Democratic excess,	$56,005 98

The only discrepancy between the total of receipts and expenditures, as given in these tables, and in the Auditor Generals' Reports, is the following: in 1858 a renewal loan of $216,000 was made, for the purpose of taking up bonds about due. This amount is included in the receipts of that year, and the bonds taken up, $197,000, included in the expenditures, and the balance, $20,000, included in the expenditures of 1859. As this transaction was simply a continuance of a debt already existing, the amount has been deducted from our exhibit of receipts and expenditures.

Aside from variances occasioned by payments upon the public debt, there has been a constant and steady increase of State expenses from year to year. This increase is a necessary consequence of the growth of the State, and the maturity of its institutions, as the comparison of a few items for a given number of years

*This includes the month of December, 1854.

will show. We give below statements of interest disbursed from the Trust Funds, (Primary School, University and Normal School,) expenses of the Judiciary, State Prison, and Tax Paying Department, for the last ten years. The latter embraces the business expenses of the Auditor General,s Department, consisting of payments to Counties on account, expenses of sales refunded and disbursed from proceeds, money refunded on redemptions, &c.

INTEREST DISBURSED FROM TRUSTFUNDS.

Democratic Rule, 5 yrs.		Republican Rule. 5 yrs.	
1850	$54,043 66	1855	$127.542 61
1851	59.034 85	1856	140.542 26
1852	71,706 40	1857	153,011 20
1853	73,353 89	1858	151.074 84
1854	110,383 31	1859	147,565 36
Total,	$368,522 11	Total,	$725.736 27
Deduct Democratic Expenditure,			368,522 11
Republican Excess,			$357,214 16

EXPENSES OF THE JUDICIARY.

Democratic Rule, 5 yrs.		Republican Rule, 5 yrs.	
1850	$9,154 83	1855	$14,900 61
1851	7,663 19	1856	16.721 29
1852	14,674 90	1857	17.945 56
1853	15,254 20	1858	25,840 10
1854	15,785 58	1859	33,542 63
Total,	$62,532 60	Total,	$108,950 19
Deduct Democratic Expenditure,			$62,532 70
Republican Excess,			$46,417 49

EXPENSES OF STATE PRISON.

Democratic Rule, 5 yrs.		Republican rule, 5 years.	
1850	$6.000 00	1855,	$16,000 00
1851	6,000 00	1856,	20,000 00
1852	9,000 00	1857,	25.000 00
1853	9,500 00	1858,	21.000 00
1854	10.500 00	1859,	13,000 00
Total,	$41,000 00	Total,	$95,000 00
Deduct Democratic expenditure,			41.000 00
Republican excess,			$54,000 00

EXPENSES OF TAX-PAYING DEPARTMENT.

Democratic rule, 5 years.		Republican rule, 5 years.	
1850,	$39,783 84	1855,	$97,437 99
1851,	43,133 40	1856,	84.313 13
1852,	44.970 23	1857,	79,632 24
1853,	73.646 75	1858,	112.904 33
1854,	87,533 65	1859,	124,775 47
Total,	$289,067 87	Total,	$499,063 16
Deduct Democratic expenditure,			289,067 87
Republican excess.			$209,995 29

Recapitulation.

Republicans paid in five years, more than was paid by Democrats for a like period, on the following items, alone:

Int. disbursed f'm T'st F'ds,	$357,214 16
Ex. of the Judiciary,	46,417 49
Ex. of State Prison,	54,000 00
Ex. of Tax-paying Department,	209,995 29
Total Rep. Exc. in 4 items,	$667,626 94

The following table completes the comparison of expenditures for the last 12 years:

EXTRAORDINARY EXPENSES.

Democratic period 7 yrs.		Repub'can. period, 5 yrs.	
1848	$115,333 61		
1849	165,338 71		
1850	129,339 00	1855	$131,691 09
1851	46,143 97	1856	142,228 11
1852,	19,071 05	1857	184,566 44
1853	23,308 76	1858	140,495 34
1854*	107,216 64	1859	163,445 67
Total,	$605.751 74	Total	$762,425 65
Deduct Democratic expenditures,			605,751 74
Republican excess			$156,673 91

BALANCES IN FAVOR OF REPUBLICAN RULE.

Let us now compare the results of the two periods mentioned, and see how the account stands:

Republican receipts, less....	$ 23.632 49
" decrease in State debt.	215.216 76
" Interest paid, excess,	119,178 87
" Extraordinary expenpenses, excess,	156,673 91
Total	$514,703 03
Deduct Dem. exc. of ord. exp.	56,005 88
Bal. in favor of Republicans,	458,697 15
Add Dem. inc. of State debt,	$240,777 19
Total balance in favor of Republican rule.....	$699,474 34

But this is quite too favorable a showing in favor of the Democracy. We gave the State debt, Dec. 1, 1847, as $2,290,768 51. But there were at that time the following resources, applicable to its payment. [See Joint Documents 1848, No. 2, page 19]:

Resources of General Fund,	$396,621 95
do Internal Imp. "	301,998 00
Total................	$698,619 95

This sum should be deducted from the amount given above, which would make the actual State debt at that time. $1,592.148 56, and would therefore add this sum of $698,619 95, to the democratic increase of the State debt.

In addition to this the sum of $63,972.46 should be deducted from the Republicon receipts for the year 1859, being the difference between the amount expended upon the Saut Canal, and the loan made exclusively for its benefit. This would make the total balance in favor of the Republicans, $1,462,066 75, or nearly one and a half millions of dollars.

FURTHER COMPARISON.

The following table exhibits the objects for which extraordinary expenses have been incurred for the past twelve years. We call your attention, fellow-citizens to the great disparity in objects

*Including December, 1854.

for which the principal expenditures have been incurred by the two parties.

ITEMS OF EXTRAORDINARY EXPFNDITURES.

	Dem. period. 7 y'rs.	Rep. period. 5 y'rs.
Const'tutional Convention,	$36,015 20	
Enlargement of State Prison,	7,249 90	$ 83.000 00
State Prison building Com'r,		3,990 00
Appropriat'ns from int. imp. fund,	379,833 44	36,442 18
Compilation of Laws,		41,175 52
Appropriations for Asylums,	29,771 74	262,570 96
Building Com'rs & Trustees of Asylums		5,187 02
Mich. State Agricultural Society,	4,800 00	10.500 00
State Agricultural School		113,994 76
House of Correction & Reform School,		78,701 46
Mich. Jour. of Education		6,074 52
Teacher's Institutes,		7,590 00
Normal School Building,	6,860 26	
Emigrant Agency,	502 50	2,214 91
Geological Survey,		2,750 00
Military purposes,	13,788 51	2,191 71
Relief of Gratiot and other counties,		11,386 21
Relief of Kansas,		1,000 00
Assessment on Asset Lands in city of Detroit (for paving),		2,715 19
Swamp Land Fund (advertising and building roads),	2,574 60	33,776 98
Saut St. Mary Canal	1,071 92	36,027 54
New Capital building, fire-proof offices and commissioner	30,278 35	455 12
Improvements at Lansing and on Great Capital Square, and removal of State offices,	11,631 69	14,312 37
Road in Houghton and Ontanagon counties,		4,000 00
Sundry appropriations,	27,071 05	2,364 20
Fraudulent awards of Board of State Auditors,	53,844 03	
Uncurrent funds,	458 55	
Total	$605,751 74	$762;426 65

Of the $379,833.44, which the Democratic party expended on appropriations for internal improvement, in addition to the legacy of $36,442.18 which they left to the Republicans, $232,500 was the amount squandered by the Legislature of 1848 in worthless appropriations, of which mention has already been made. It will be seen that the Republican party, in five years, have contributed to educational, agricultural, and charitable purposes, the sum of $497,004.93, while the Democracy, during seven years of their rule, applied to all these objects only the paltry sum of $41,432 ! ! The sum of $53,844.03, fraudulent awards, was principally expended during the last month of Democratic administrations, and consists of the following items :

Geo. W. Peck, double pay, award, Aug. 18, 1853,	$450 00
C. J. Fox, *et al.*, timber agency and sham suits, awards, 1854,	3,275 32
Gilbert & Co., award, Dec. 2, 1854,	2,204 29
Phœnix Bank, do	35,603 74
Job Brookfield, do	4,000 00
Geo. W. Peck, constructive printing, award, Dec. 29, 1854,	999 90
S. D. Elwood & Co., flat cap never delivered, award, Dec. 30, 1854,	1,076 00
Bronson, Knight & Ingalls, award, Dec. 30, 1854,	6,234 78
Total,	$53,844 03

With this record staring them in the face, the Democracy have the brazen effrontery to prate about the profligacy and corruption of the Republican party, and ask you to restore them to power, that they may re-inaugurate the policy to which they have invariably adhered when in power. If you believe in wholesale robbery, theft, fraud, profligacy and extravagance, and desire to renew their sway in Michigan, you have only to restore the Democratic party to power, and your desire will be abundantly gratified.

CONSTRUCTIVE PRINTING.

The award to Geo. W. Peck for constructive printing was not only a fraud, but a direct violation of the Constitution of the State. The Constitution, Art. IV., Sec. 22, declares that "the Legislature shall prescribe by law the manner in which the State printing shall be executed, and the accounts rendered therefor ; *and shall prohibit all charges for constructive labor.*" The following is a transcript of the vouchers upon which Mr. Peck drew pay for constructive printing :

STATE OF MICHIGAN, per Sec. of State.
To GEO. W. PECK, DR.
1854.
Dec. 23. To printing census statistics, &c., 1854; composition, 3,030,000 ems, at 33c, ... $999 90
Endorsed "Allowed and paid Dec. 29, 1854."

Here follows another voucher which includes pay for exactly the *same work* at exactly the same price—there being only *one composition* for the same charges for printing :

STATE OF MICHIGAN, per State Ag. Soc.,
To GEO. W. PECK. DR.
1854.
Dec. 23. To printing Report of Mich. State Ag. Society; composition, 4,858,770 ems, at 33c, ... $1,603 39
Endorsed correct, and paid Dec. 29. 1854.

The amount of $999.90 was here allowed in the second voucher, after having been paid in the first—the census statistics being included in the report of the State Agricultural Society. This sum, which justly belongs to the Treasury, was fraudulently paid over to a political partisan, upon a false voucher, for *constructive* printing, expressly *prohibited* by the Constitution !

INTEREST UPON CASH BALANCES IN THE TREASURY.

The Democracy have loudly boasted of the large amount kept on hand in the Treasury by themselves, and seek to cast odium upon the Republicans because as large an amount is not kept on hand at the present time. The policy of keeping large cash balances in the Treasury is commented upon by Governor Parsons, in his message to the Legislature of 1855, in the following language: "A large surplus in the Treasury should be avoided. It is not politic to tax the people to obtain money to loan to banks, or lock up in the Treasury vaults; it would be safer in the people's hands, and likely to be more prudently and profitably managed by them." The following are the yearly cash balances in the Treasury since 1842:

TABLE showing the cash balances in the Treasury at the commencement of each of the following fiscal years, (see Auditor Generals' Reports,) except the year 1855, in which we give the amount in the Treasury on the accession of the Republican party to power.

Democratic rule.		Republican rule.	
1842,	$83,726 82	1855,	$468,893 39
1843,	70,522 29	1856,	516,475 15
1844,	85,789 55	1857,	387.968 04
1845,	36,424 97	1858,	158,642 70
1846,	18,892 81	1859,	176,347 20
1847,	78,561 00		
1848,	62,304 45		
1849,	51,681 55		
1850,	55,447 39		
1851,	35,044 27		
1852,	97,243 23		
1853,	116,407 23		
1854,	375,625 70		
Aggregate	$1,167,671 26	Aggregate	$1,708,326 48

It will be seen that at the commencement of the fiscal year 1846, the cash balance in the Treasury was only $18,892 81! When it reaches that figure under Republican rule, it will be ample time for the fierce democracy to begin to howl.

Upon an aggregate cash balance of $1,708,326 48 the Republicans have received the sum of $71,338 61 in five years, as interest for its use. A proportionate sum upon the aggregate for the democratic period given above, would, without regard to time, amount to $49,104 10. This amount, at least, should have been received into the Treasury, as interest upon cash balances during that long period of thirteen years. But, as we have already stated, the only amount the democrats ever paid into the Treasury for the use of cash balances, was the sum of $1,553 86! Here, then is a swindle of $47,550 24! !

Yet these Democratic patriots, who have such terrible convulsions over a loss which has never been incurred by the State, had not a word of condemnation for this gross violation of duty!

GOVERNMENT STOCK BANK FRAUD.

The law required the bills of the Government Stock Bank to be countersigned by the State Treasurer, and that no bills should be put in circulation except their full value was secured by stocks deposited in the Treasury. Consequently the over-issue of these bills which occurred, was a base fraud, perpetuated by the State Treasurer, his Deputy, or others, who had access to the vaults of the State. Under Republican rule, all surrendered bills of State banks are immediately burned in the presence of the person making the surrender. Had this manifest duty been performed under democratic rule, no over-issue of the circulating notes of the Government Stock Bank would have occurred. Instead of this being done, they were *not even mutilated*, but were suffered to remain scattered about on shelves and other convenient places, from which they could be stolen and put again in circulation.

According to a notice previously given by the State Treasurer, upon which the surrender of these bills was made, the dividend was declared on the 3d day of July, 1855. The amount given in the following tables as outstanding, was bills which were surrendered subsequently to the declaration of the dividend, and were consequently a total loss to the holders:

		Dead Loss.
Circulat'g N't's surrend'd,	$95,425 25	
Dividend paid on same	38,170 10	$57,255 15
Amount Outstanding		15,000 00
Total Loss		$72,255 15

Here, then, in this one item alone, the democratic party robbed the people of $72,255 15! !

OTHER RAIL ROAD LOANS.

The amount sunk in the loan to the Pontiac Railroad Company was by no means the entire loss incurred by loans to railroads. Gov. Ransom, in his message to the Legislature of 1849, (page 25,) says:

> "The policy of loaning the money or credit of the State to corporations, has almost universally proved disastrous to the interests of the State. Our own past experienee is full of instruction on this subject. This policy formed a prominent feature in our original system of internal improvment. The credit of the State was loaned to various railroad companies, to a very large amount, which resulted in a certain loss of more than THREE HUNDRED THOUSAND DOLLARS, *every dollar of which is yet to be wrung from the pockets of the people by the hands of the tax gatherer.*"

Deduct from this sum the amount lost by the Pontiac Rail Road loan, and we have, as the loss in loans to other railroads, the sum of $115,000!

THE SWEGLES FRAUD.

In the fall of 1857, duplicate part-pald bonds, to the amount of $4,000, were sent to the State Treasurer for payment of interest thereon. After considerable investigation, it was ascertained that these bonds had been issued by "honest!" John Swegles, and that he had received their cash value, $2,269 40. On being charged with the crime, this *honest* democrat official confessed it, and might at any time be incarcerated within the State prison, for this robbery of the State.

GRAND RECAPITULATION ! ! !

The people's money which has been squandered, lost or stolen by the democratic party.

Loss on sale of Central and Southern Railroads, and on abandoned public works................	$1,720,433 71
Loss on Pontiac Railroad Loan.................	185,000 00
Loss on other Railr'd Loans	115,000 00
" on in't on Cash Balances,	47,550 24
Amount stolen from the Primary School and University Funds...........	71,725 16
Grv. Stock Bank frrud....	72,255 15
Fraudulent awards of 1853 and 1854..............	53,794 03
Fraudulent re-issue of bonds,	2,269 40
Uncurrent Funds.........	458 55
	$2,268,486 24

We have only included in this statement such instances of democratic imbecility and corruption as are indisputably proven by public records. Neither have we added interest upon the amounts, but have only given the orignal loss. Had we included all obvious cases of fraud, and reckoned interes to the present time upon each original loss, the aggregage would have swollen to the enormous sum of over **$5,000,000 00 ! !**

TAXATION FOR THE EXPENSES OF STATE GOVERNMENT.

The sham democracy have attempted to realize a little capital by misrepresentation of the following extracts :

"The State is perfectly free from embarrassments in her financial condition, and it is believed that by the practice of a proper system of economy, no resort to a system of direct taxation will be required to meed the ordinary expenses of the government."—*Gov. Bingham's Inaugural*, 1855.

"The large surplus in the Treasury, with the income from specific taxes and the sale of State lands, it is believed, will be found sufficient to defray the ordinary expenses of the government."—*Auditor Jone's Report*, 1855.

We append the following table, in order that intelligent men may be able to judge how much of the State taxes that have been levied under Republican rule, have really been "required to meet the *ordinary* expenses of the government :"

Appropriations Legislature 1855.

For Asylums.............		$100,000 00
For House of Correction,...		25,000 00
For enlargem'nt State Prison		44,000 00
Total................		$169,000 00
State tax, 1855,..	40,000	
" 1856,..	65,000	
		$105,000 00
Excess of appropriations for above objects,..........		$64,000 00

Appropriations Legislature 1857.

For Asylum,..............		$125,000 00
For House of Correction,...		33,773 76
For Agricultnral College,.....		40,000 00
For enlargem't State Prison,		32,000 00
Total, ...		$230,773 76
State tax, 1857..	$85,065 20	
" 1858..	85,065 20	
		170,130 40
Excess of appropriations....		$60,643 36

Appropriations Legislature 1859.

For Asylums,.............		$182,500 00
For House of Correction....		20,000 00
For Agricultnral College,..		37,500 00
For enlargement State Pris'n		27,000 00
Relief of Gratiot County,...		15,000 00
Total,...............		$282,000 00
State tax, 1859,..	202,663 00	
" 1860,..	154,663 00	
		$357,326 00

Recapitulation.

Aggregate appropriations during six years of Republican rule, for the above items alone, ...	$681,773 76
Aggregate State Taxes during six years of Republican rule,......	632,456 40
Excess of appropriations,..	$49,317 36

As will be seen, this statement includes only the largest items of appropriations.

DEMOCRATIC CHARGES.

Among the numerous false and ridiculous charges made against the Republican party, we find the following :

"The Republican party, during five years of its rule, increased the liabilities of the State one million one hundred and forty-eight thousand, seven hundred and thirty-four dollars and ninety-one cents." —*Lansing Journal.*

As a matter of curiosity, we will show how so absurd a result is reached.

In the first place, the amount of Republican reduction of the State debt is whittled down to a mere cypher. Then to this is added the amount due the trust funds—*principal and interest*; the Saut Canal loan of $100,000; the renewal and temporary loans of 1858, which appear in the account of State indebtedness; and also the balance due counties on account with the Auditor General. The only one of these items necessary to explain here is the last one mentioned. All lands in the different counties, on which the taxes remain unpaid, are returned to the office of the Auditor General, and on such return, the amount of taxes due is credited to the several counties. When such taxes are paid, or the lands are sold, the counties are entitled to receive the amount credited to them, after deducting their apportioned amount of State tax, and not before. To charge this amount due the counties as one of the "liabilities of the State," is therefore supremely ridiculous. By such a queer system of double entry and false charges, the sham democracy arrive at the astounding result we have quoted.

The wonder is that they should stop at the sum they have specified; for by such a liberal disregard of facts and sense, they might have made the amount almost any sum they chose.

THAT FIFTY THOUSAND DOLLARS.

One of the principal arguments which the Democratic politicians employ in this campaign, is the charge that the Republicans have lost $50,000 of the Saut Canal loan. In order to place this matter in its proper light, and also to quiet the apprehensions of these sensitive individuals, we copy the following truthful statement of the Detroit *Tribune*, with rarard to the securities obtained for this sum:

"A full report has been received from a competent person employed to make an abstract of the title to the lands included in the mortgage executed by Geo. M. Dewey and E. H. Hazleton to the State of Michigan, for the collateral security of the $50,000 of the Saut Ste Marie's Canal loan above mentioned.

"The mortgage covers 13,440 acres of lands situated mainly in Genesee, Saginaw, Midland and Tuscola counties.

"Over 6,000 acres of these lands were located in 1836, known as the 'Brent lands,' and are among the most valuable timbered and unimproved lands in the county of Genesee. These lands alone are worth at a cash valuation more than the amount of the mortgage, as is well known to the writer of this, from a personal knowledge of many years of the lands in question. There can, therefore, no longer remain a doubt as to the ultimate security of the $50,000 due the State upon this loan.

"It gives us pleasure to make this announcement, the more, because we have been among those who have heretofore placed very little confidence in the value of the security in question."

DEMOCRATIC NON-PAYMENT OF INTEREST.

The Democracy are wont to boast of the large amount they kept on hand in the Treasury, and left to the Republican party; notwithstanding the keeping of a large sum in the Treasury was regarded by Gov. Parsons as detrimental to the interests of the State. But had they performed their duty in the single matter of the payment of interest upon the State debt, which they left unpaid during only the last five years of their rule, the amount they would have left on hand in the Treasury, when they went out of power, would have been *slightly* reduced; as the following exhibit shows:

INTEREST LEFT UNPAID BY DEMOCRATS DURING THE LAST FIVE YEARS OF THEIR RULE.

In 1850 they left unpaid....	$96,500 00
1851 " "	93,000 00
1852 " "	92,600 00
1853 " "	94,800 00
1854 " "	94,000 00
Total................	$470,900 00
Cash on hand, January 1st, 1855..................	468,893 39
Excess of Interest left unpaid in 5 years........	2,006 61

Thus we see that, if they had performed this obvious duty of paying the interest upon the State debt, for only the last five years of their rule, there would have been $2,006 61 minus a red cent in the Treasury on the first day of January, 1855.

STATE TAXES.

As the locofoco party raise a great cry about the burden of State taxes with which the Republican party have borne down the people, we invite their attention to a comparison of the five years of

Republican rule with an equal number of years of Democratic rule:

Comparison of the Rate of Tax upon the Dollar during five years of Democratic and Five Years of Republican rule.

Democratic Rule.		Republican Rule.	
YEAR	MILLS	YEAR	MILLS
1848	5.04	1855	0.33
1849	3.53	1856	0.47
1850	3.86	1857	0.61
1851	3.42	1858	0.61
1852	3.55	1859	1.47

Let us illustrate: In 1848, a man worth $1,000 had to pay a State tax of $5 04, and in 1855 his tax was $0 33!! In 1851, at the lowest rate of these five years of Democratic rule, his tax was $3-42, and in 1859, at the *highest* rate of the five years of Republican rule, his tax was only $1 47!! This must be plain to the most obtuse mind.

Now let us take another view of the subject. The aggregate State valuation from the year 1848 to the year 1852, inclusive, was $150,244,781. The aggregate State tax for the same time was $582,893. The aggregate State valuation from the year 1855 to the year 1859, inclusive, was 671,014,510. The aggregate State tax for the same time was $477,793. Thus we see that during five years of Democratic rule, upon an aggregate property valuation of the State of $520,769,729 *less*, they assessed an aggregate State tax of $105,100 GREATER, than has been levied during five years of Republican rule! Had the Republican party during the past five years, oppressed the people of Michigan with a State tax proportionate to that which they had to bear upon the property valuation during the five previous years mentioned, they would have compelled them to pay the round sum of

$2,603,216 28!

THE SAUT CANAL.

The subject of the Saut canal, and the loan made for its benefit, has excited considerable attention. As this question has been pretty thoroughly discussed, we only propose to call your attention to a single point made by democratic stump orators. It is this: They state that, if the loan of $100,000 had not been made, all the large amount of tolls, necessary to be collected for its payment, would have flowed into the Treasury of the State, and would thus have furnished funds which must be drawn from the pockets of the people. In order to put down this falsehood, it is only necessary to quote the Act of Congress making the grant of land for the construction of the canal. The act says:

"The legislature of said State shall cause to be kept an accurate account * * * of all expenditures in the construction, *repairs and operating* of said Canal, and of thr earnings thereof; * * * and whenever said State shall be fully reimbursed for all *advances* made for the construction, repairs and operating of said Canal, with legal interest on all *advances*, * * * the said State shall be allowed to tax for the use of said Canal *only such tolls as shall be sufficient to pay all necessary expenses for the care, charge and repairs of the same.*"

THE YEAR 1853.

This was an extraordinary year in the financial history of Michigan. That year the State Tax was only $10,000 00! The democracy never tire of parading this fact before the people. No person, by reading democratic papers, would be informed that any State Tax was ever raised previous to that time, as in all their statements on the subject they never go back of that $10,000. In all their estimates of the increase of State taxes they invariably commence with that 10,000 00!

But let us look at the facts connected with their financial management of the affairs of the State during that year, and see if they furnish anything of which the Democracy can boast.

The Constitution of the State, Art. XIV, Sec. 1, says: "The Legislature shall provide for an *annual tax*, sufficient, with other resources, to pay the estimated expenses of the State Government, the interest of the State debt, and such deficiency as may occur in the resources."

We give below a statement of the current expenses of the year 1853, comprehended by this clause of the Constitution, and the resources applicable to the payment of said expenses:

TABLE showing the current expenses of the State for the year 1853, and the resources applicable to the payment thereof.

CURRENT EXPENSES.

Salaries of public officers,....	$12,959 07
Expenses of Legislature, 1853,	21,148 23
" State prison,....	9,500 00
" Supreme Court,.	15,254 20
Interest on State indebtedness,	173,050 44
Total,..................	$231,911 94

RESOURCES.

Specific taxes,..............	$96,018 43

U. S. 5 per cents,	10,328 17
State tax,	10,000 00
Total,	$116,346 60

RECAPITULATION.

Current expenses,	$231,911 94
Resources,	116,346 60
Amount unprovided for,	$115,565 34

Here, then, is a legacy of $115,565.34 left to the people of the State in direct violation of one of the plainest provisions of the Constitution—left, too, by the Democratic party in that wonderful year of our Lord, 1853!

ANOTHER DEMOCRATIC VIOLATION OF THE CONSTITUTION.

Among other provisions of the Democratic Constitution of 1850, is one (Art. XIV., Sec. 2,) which declares that "the Legislature shall provide by law a sinking fund of at least $20,000 a year, to commence in 1852, with compound interest at the rate of six per cent. per annum, and an annual increase of at least five per cent., to be applied solely to the payment and extinguishment of the State debt."

Yet this model Democratic party made no provision whatever to comply with this requirement of a Constitution made exclusively by themselves! It is to be regretted that the change of administration did not occur until this provision had been rendered inoperative by Democratic neglect.

We give the following estimate for ten years, from the report of Auditor General John J. Adam, Dec. 1, 1850, of the amount of State tax necessary to be levied to pay the interest upon the State debt, and to provide for the liquidation of the principal as it should fall due:

TOTAL TAX FOR INTEREST AND PRINCIPAL OF STATE DEBT.

YEAR.	TAX.	YEAR.	TAX.
1852,	$140.000 00	1857,	$146,227 80
1853,	141,000 00	1858,	147 912 86
1854,	142,110 00	1859,	149,783 27
1855,	143,342 10	1860,	151,859 43
1856,	144,709 73	1861,	154,163 97

Mr. Adam's estimate for the payment of these two items goes on increasing from year to year, until 1875, when it reaches the sum of $231,147.91!! We commend these figures to the consideration of those who have brawled so vociferously about „Taxes! Taxes!! Taxes!!!"

APPEAL.

Fellow citizens! our cause is before you. Conscious of the rectitude of our principles, the correctness of our policy, and the ability, integrity and fitness of our candidates—State and national, we present them to you with the fullest confidence of your cordial and hearty support.

We have dwelt at length upon matters of State finance, not because of their overshadowing importance, but because we would stop the mouths of those who desire to draw your attention from the vital issues that press upon your consideration.

Questions of greater importance than these meet each other face to face in this contest, and demand a solution at your hands. As the fathers stood, in the trying days of the Revolution, manfully up to their duties to their country, to humanity and to God, so you are called upon to stand, amid the political revolution of to-day, and by an earnest yet peaceful struggle in behalf of the same principles for which they pledged their "lives, their fortunes, and their sacred honor," prove that you are worthy sons of noble sires! The errors of the past, whatever they may have been, must rest with their authors; but the future of this country is your own. It has as yet but just entered upon its career of greatness, and the woof of its destiny is almost unwoven.

By preserving sacred to freedom the vast inheritance that lies a mighty, unoccupied empire on our western border, you will lay the foundation of a greatness, prosperity and endurance that will exceed the hardihood of Rome, the glory of Greece, the serenity of Carthage!

The name of our republic has become the rallying cry of freedom in all lands, and no man who loves her fame, or cherishes her welfare, will deface those principles from her escutcheon which have given her prosperity, prestige, and immortal renown.

Republicans! the thickening evidences of the success of our principles should nerve your arms and strengthen your hearts for the closing struggle! Already, in the midst of the contest, the green hills of Vermont send forth her thunders of victory, that roll to the remotest verge of the republic!

Scarce have the footsteps of this mighty peal passed across the heavens, ere the "rocking pines" of Maine, from all their deep recesses, give back the glorious and swelling anthem of triumph!

Our enemies see the hand-writing on the wall, and like the imbecile king of old, their knees smite together! They have scoffed at and defied the "higher law," and ignored and denied the "irrepressible conflict," yet the higher law, which works out the grand results of justice, has undermined the foundation of wrong upon which they have built; while the irrepressible conflict between truth and error, right and wrong, which they have so long derided, has penetrated to their very vitals and rent them in twain! Verily, "whom the Gods would destroy they first make mad!" In all these events which are transpiring before our eyes, we see the wonder-workings of that overruling Hand that leads the nations by paths they have not trodden, and that brings joyous and beneficent results out of evils that have too long afflicted the world.

Let not victory cause you to relax your efforts, nor the dissensions of your foes lull you to security, but let each incite you to more vigorous and determined action. It is only by eternal vigilance that liberty can triumph, or her triumph be maintained. And if, in the coming contest, prejudice, treachery, or fraud, shall accomplish our defeat, be not disheartened. The Republican party will still live, for its principles are life-giving; and victory must sooner or later attend its onward march; for

"Freedom's battle once begun,
Bequeathed from bleeding sire to son,
Though baffled oft, is ever won!"

I. M. CRAVATH,
HORACE ANGELL,
JOHN DUNSBACK,
Ex. Com. of Ingham Co. Rep. Cen'l Com.
I. H. BARTHOLOMEW, Sec'y.
Lansing, Sept. 13, 1860.

TO THE REPUBLICAN ELECTORS OF KALAMAZOO COUNTY.

Your County Committee, with pleasure, indorse the above clear and able expose of our State Finances. We have carefully examined it, and believe it to be true in every particular. We bespeak for it a careful perusal by every Republican in the County. Read it, study it, and *with it* prove to your Democratic friends and neighbors that our State is not bankrupt, that its finances are in a prosperous condition, and that both the State and its finances are still safe in the hands of the Republican Party.

Your Committee have taken measures so that every voter in the County may have a copy of this valuable document; and that, hereafter, no person will have any excuse for deceiving or being deceived in reference to the present financial condition of our Sta e.

DWIGHT MAY,
E. R. MILLER,
CHAS. T. RICHARDSON.
Oct. 16th, 1860. Co. Com.

From the Daily Telegraph, Oct. 15.

DOUGLAS'S ADVENT.

To-morrow Senator Douglas speaks to the "citizens of Kalamazoo and vicinity on the political topics of the day." What he will say it may or may not be easy to tell; what he *has* said in a hundred places is before the country. Of this much we may be certain—he will carefully consult the latitude of the place in which he speaks, and temper his sentiments to the prevailing opinion of his auditory. This piece which he recites is variously tuned to suit the dissimilar tympana of the crowds which he has addressed in such separate localities—for it is evident that "Democracy" is not quite the same everywhere, and Douglas strives to be a "Democrat" everywhere. Here where Free-Soil STUART is domiciled, and Free Labor sentiments grow rank, his lyre will probably be tuned to Anti-Slavery concert pitch, and so our townsmen will hear but the one commendable strain. But that lyre has a thousand strings, and that tune has a hundred variations, and for fear that the crowd on Tuesday will have no opportunity of hearing all of Douglas's performances, and the many changes he can get out of that good old recitative—"My Principle,"—we publish below a number of the variations which have struck his various audiences with so much admiration. Read carefully and see if the Little Giant can't turn his hand to almost everything:

January 23, 1860, in the Senate, Douglas said:

"IF I WAS A CITIZEN OF LOUISIANA I WOULD VOTE FOR RETAINING SLAVERY BECAUSE I BELIEVE THE GOOD OF THAT PEOPLE WOULD REQUIRE IT."—*Congressional Globe*, 1859-60; *page* 559.

At Memphis, Tenn., November 29th, 1858, as reported in the *Avelanche*, of that city, he said:

"The Almighty has drawn the line on this continent ON ONE SIDE OF WHICH THE SOIL MUST BE CULTIVATED BY SLAVE LABOR."

If this be not a straightforward statement that the Almighty requires the existence and perpetuation of slavery, we do not read it aright. O, yes, he is opposed to slavery as much as any one!

When the Toombs bill was under consideration in the Senate, Senator Trumbull offered an amendment, giving the *people* of Kansas power to *exclude* slavery. Douglas, popular sovereignty man that he is, (and Stuart, too,) *voted this down*, and thus explains his vote:

"*If the Constitution carries slavery there, let it go, and no power on earth can take it away.*"

Where is "my great principle" now?

In New Orleans, Dec. 6, 1858, he said:

"*Slaves are recognized as property, and placed on an equal footing with all other property. Hence, the owner of slaves—the same as the owner of any other species of property—has a right to remove to a Territory and carry his property with him.*"

In the Senate, on the 23d of February, 1859, he said:

"I do not put slavery on a different footing from other property. I recognize it as property under what is understood to be the decision of the Supreme Court. I recognize slave property to be *on an equality with all other property*, and apply the same rules to it. I will not apply one rule to slave property and another to all other kinds of property.—*Congressional Globe*, 1858–9, *part* 2, *page* 1256.

And again:

"Slaves according to that decision, being property, stand on an equal footing with all other property. THERE IS JUST AS MUCH OBLIGATION ON THE PART OF THE TERRITORIAL LEGISLATURE to PROTECT SLAVES AS EVERY OTHER SPECIES OF PROPERTY, AS THERE IS TO PROTECT HORSES, CATTLE, DRY GOODS, LIQUORS, &c."—*Congressional Globe, same vol., page* 1258.

In his letter replying to Judge Black, published in *Harper's Magazine*, he said:

"In that article, without assailing any one, or impugning any man's motive, I demonstrated, beyond the possibility of cavil or dispute, if slavery exists in the Territories by virtue of the Constitution, the conclusion is inevitable and irresistible, THAT IT IS THE IMPERATIVE DUTY OF CONGRESS TO PASS ALL LAWS NECESSARY FOR ITS PROTECTION; THAT THERE IS AND CAN BE NO EXCEPTION TO THE RULE, THAT A RIGHT GUARANTEED BY THE CONSTITUTION MUST BE PROTECTED BY LAW IN ALL CASES WHERE LEGISLATION IS ESSENTIAL TO ITS ENJOYMENT."

And he goes on further to say:

"All who believe that slavery exists in the Territories by virtue of the Constitution, are bound by their consciences and their oaths of fidelity to the Constitution, TO SUPPORT A SLAVE CODE FOR THE TERRITORIES."

The "Wickliffe" resolution of the Baltimore Platform, and consequently part of the creed of Douglas Democrats, is the following:

"*Resolved*, That it is in accordance with the Cincinnati platform, that during the existence of Territorial Governments, the measure of restriction, whatever it may be, imposed by the Federal Constitution on the power of the Territorial Legislature over the subject of the domestic relations *as the same has been or shall hereafter be decided by the Supreme Court* of the United States, should be respected by all good citizens and enforced with promptness and fidelity by every branch of the General government."

On this straightforward slave code resolve, Mr. Douglas remarks in his letter of acceptance, dated Washington, June 29, 1860;

"Upon a careful examination of the platform of principles adopted at Cha'ston, and re-affirmed at Baltimore, with an additional resolution which is in perfect harmony with the others, I find it to be a faithful embodiment of the time-honored principles of the Democratic party, as the same were proclaimed and understood by all parties in the Presidential contests of 1848, 1852 and 1856."

In the Senate, 1855, he said:

"I am for a reduction of the tariff to a strict revenue standard. I am a free-trade man to the fullest extent that we can carry it."

And in his recent speech at Harrisburg, he said, of Pennsylvania:

"Her interests required the fostering hand of government. *The system of government must change or disaster would occur. THE ONLY REMEDY IS A PROPER TARIFF.*"

"Which is who?" In a speech in the Senate, he said:

"No man can vindicate the character, the motives and the conduct of the Declaration of Independence, except upon the hypothesis that they referred to the white race alone, and not to the African, when they declared all men to have been created free and equal—that they were speaking of *British subjects* on this continent being equal to British subjects born and residing in Great Britain—that they were entitled to the same inalienable rights, and among them were enumerated life, liberty, and the pursuit of happiness. The Declaration of Independence was adopted merely for the purpose of justifying the colonists in the eyes of the civilized world in withdrawing their allegiance from the British crown, and dissolving their connection with the mother country."

Oh, lame and impotent conclusion!—was it for nothing higher or nobler than that, a seven years bloody struggle was endured? And what of the oppressed millions of Europe who have since sought a refuge and a home on this continent?

From the Daily Telegraph, Oct. 16.

THEY DON'T TELL ALL.

Among the many banners and flags paraded to-day we do not see one of Johnson's peculiar sentiments exposed. This is all wrong, and we fear that the excellent committee who had the entire charge of getting up the very pretty show of the day, were careless in this particular, though watchful and happy in many of their arrangements. We wish to remedy their neglect, and so supply some of their omissions:

Mr. Herschel V. Johnson, Douglas candidate for Vice President, is also a "popular sovereignty" man, but he is less of a demagogue than Douglas, and rests his doctrine entirely on the Dred Scott decision, without ambiguity, and therefore, July 7, 1848, in the Senate, he said:

"It matters not where the power of legislating for the Territory resides—exclusively in Congress, or jointly in Congress and the inhabitants, or exclusively in the inhabitants of the Territory; the power is precisely the same—no greater in the hands of one than the other. *In no event* can the slaveholder of the South be excluded from settling in such Territory WITH HIS PROPERTY OF EVERY DESCRIPTION.—*Cong. Globe Appendix*, 1847, '48; *p.* 891.

But see how he crushes out "popular sovereignty:"

"But suppose that Congress have the right to establish a Territorial Govenment only, and that then all further governmental control ceases; can the Territorial Legislature *pass an act prohibiting Slavery? Surely not!* * * * If therefore the act of a Territorial Government prohibiting Slavery, should be sent up to Congress for approval, *they would be bound* to withhold it, upon the ground of its being an act which Congress themselves could not pass.—*Cong. Globe, same vol. and p.*

In a letter dated May 28, 1860, addressed to a Southern gentleman, and published in the Southern papers, Mr. Johnson says:

"☞ I believe that it is the right of " the South to demand, and the duty of " Congress to extend, protection of person " and property of every kind (including " slavery) in the Territories during their " Territorial state. This is no new opinion. I advocated this doctrine as far back as 1848, in the Senate of the United States.

On the 30th of August, 1851, Mr. Johnson wrote a letter to certain gentlemen who had invited him to attend a "Southern Rights" barbacue in honor of Col. Robert McMillen, in which he took the most revolutionary grounds concerning the rights of Georgia to secede from the Union. He said:

☞ "The great issue, then, I repeat, is the right of a State to secede from the Union, and the correlative absence of any right, on the part of the Federal Government to force such a State back into the Union. It cannot be evaded by THE SENSLESS CLAMOR OF UNION! THIS GLORIONS UNION!

* * * * * *

"Whoever observes the signs of the times cannot fail to see that the RIGHT OF SECESSION will probably, AT NO DISTANT DAY, ASSUME THE FORM AND MAGNITUDE OF A PRACTICAL IMPORTANCE."

"THE RIGHT OF SECESSION

MUST BE MAINTAINED. IT IS THE LAST, THE ONLY HOPE OF THE SOUTH."

Will Douglas now talk much about the danger of this Union, if any other than his and Johnson's party succeeds?

But Johnson also says:

"It is urged that slavery does not exist in New Mexico and California; that they are free territories; and although we deny to Congress any jurisdiction over the subject, *yet we ask Congress by this amendment to establish Slavery therein.*"

And what do the hard-fisted yeomanry who carry the banners bearing his name think of these his sentiments?

"We believe that capital should *own* labor."

Mr. Johnson could not let the opportunity slip of insulting the working men of the North, in his recent speech at Pittsburg. He denounced them as "slaves"—as men "owned by their employers;" varying his favorite theory that "capital SHOULD own labor," by asserting that capital DOES own it. In speaking of slavery, (we copy from the Gazette's report,) he said:

"LOOK AT THE SLAVES IN YOUR OWN WORKSHOPS! THEY ARE DRIVEN TO THE POLL AT THE BECK OF THEIR MASTERS, UNDER PENALTY OF BEING DISCHARGED!"

"This," says the Gazette, "was received with indignant cries of "Not so!" 'No, sir!" "No, no!" "No, sir-ree, bob!" and so on, the workmen in the crowd giving the insulting falsehood the most emphatic denial. A voice in the crowd asked, "What about Capital owning Labor?" He answered by repeating the insult, in substance: "I do not believe," he said, "in one white man owning another, as the masters in your workshops do!"

☞ Herschel V. Johnson said, in his speech at Terre Haute, "Abe Lincoln, the great Rail-Splitter—I own twenty boys (negroes); any one can beat him at a day's work splitting rails, and give two hundred. I would prefer one of them for President, so help me God, to Abe Lincoln."

TO THE REPUBLICAN ELECTORS OF KALAMAZOO COUNTY:

The Republican County Committee make the following appointments for Republican meetings at the several places indicated. The friends of the cause in the several localities, are requested to give the speakers a generous welcome.—Let Old Kalamazoo indorse the nomination of LINCOLN and BLAIR by thousands.

By order of the Com.

HON. STEPHEN F. BROWN'S APPOINTMENTS.

Oct. 18, Alamo Centre, evening
" 19, Schoolcraft.
" 20, Portage, Durkee's Sch. house, evening.
" 23, Wakeshma, afternoon.
" 24, Augusta, evening.
" 26, Cooper Centre, evening.
" 27, Vicksburgh, "
" 29, Climax Corners, "
" 31, Richland Centre "
Nov. 2, Galesburgh, "
" 5, Kalamazoo.

HON. MARSH GIDDINGS' APPOINTMENTS.

Oct. 19, Schoolcraft,
" 22, Galesburgh, evening.
" 24, Yorkville, "
" 26, Alamo Centre, "
" 29, Texas, at Towers' School house, evening,
Oct. 31, Cooper Centre, "
Nov. 2, Cooper, at Vradenberg's School house, in the evening.
Nov. 5, Kalamazoo.

CHAS. S. MAY'S APPOINTMENTS.

Oct. 15, Cooper Centre, evening.
" 17, Texas, Towers' sch. h., eve.
" 19, Oshtemo, Hind's sch. house evening.
Oct. 22, Climax Corners, evening.
" 24, Portage, Carpenter's Corners, evening.
" 26, Prairie Ronde, Harrison's school house, evening.
Oct. 29, Pavillion, McKain's school house, evening,
Oct. 31, Comstock, evening.
Nov. 1, Schoolcraft, "
" 5, Kalamazoo "

DR. E. C. ADAMS' APPOINTMENTS.

Oct. 11, Cooper Centre, evening.
" 13, Alamo, Carrier's sch. house, evening.
" 17, Cooper, at Vradenburg school house, evening.
Oct. 19, Texas, Keyser sch. house, eve.
Nov. 5, Kalamazoo.

www.ingramcontent.com/pod-product-compliance
Lightning Source LLC
LaVergne TN
LVHW020638110826
845149LV00004B/1269
9781418190194